SIMON AND SCHUSTER
BOOKS FOR YOUNG READERS
Simon & Schuster Building,
Rockefeller Center,
1230 Avenue of the Americas,
New York, New York 10020.

Text copyright © 1989 by Eve Merriam
Illustrations copyright © 1989 by Eugenie Fernandes
SIMON AND SCHUSTER BOOKS FOR YOUNG READERS
is a trademark of Simon & Schuster Inc.
Manufactured in the United States of America

10 9 8 7 6 5 4 3 2

Library of Congress Cataloging-in-Publication Data
Merriam, Eve . Daddies at work. Summary: Portrays
daddies in different jobs, including sailor daddies, tailor
daddies, and lawyer daddies with egg salad sandwiches in
their briefcases. [1. Occupations. 2. Fathers—
Employment.] I. Eugenie, ill. II. Title.
HF5381.M399 1989   88-19799
ISBN 0-671-64873-X

#4593
6/90
$5.95
232ff
re-cat 6/95
381796000544112

Daddies at Work

by Eve Merriam • Illustrated by Eugenie Fernandes

Simon and Schuster Books for Young Readers
Published by Simon & Schuster Inc.,
New York

Daddies lift you up and swing you around.

Daddies tickle you
with their beards.

Daddies sing silly songs.

Daddies make spaghetti messes.

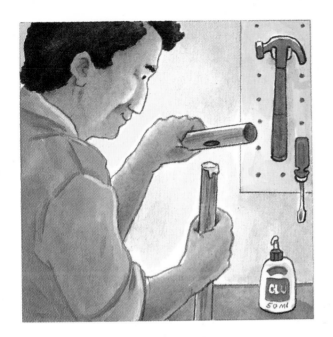

Daddies fix toys that are broken.

Daddies read stories and bring glasses of water.

What other things do daddies do?

All kinds of daddies at all kinds of jobs.

Bus driver daddies.

Carpenter daddies.

Daddies who are doctors.

Daddies who are nurses.

Daddies on fire trucks.

Daddies in parades.

Daddies in tree tops.

Daddies digging holes.

Daddies in the clouds.

Tailor daddies and sailor daddies.

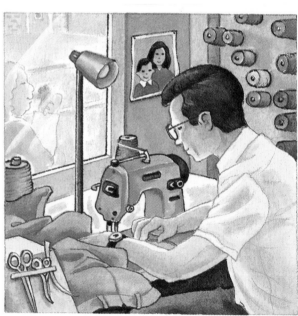

Daddies on horseback.

Hair cutting daddies.

Computer daddies.

Lawyer daddies with egg salad sandwiches in their briefcases.

Laundromat daddies.

Waiter daddies.

Painter daddies.

Umpire daddies.

Daddies working in hotels

and stores and zoos.

Fat daddies,
thin daddies.

Short, tall,
in between
daddies.

Daddies with mustaches

and daddies who are bald . . .

and all daddies everywhere

loving the most of all to be your very own daddy,
and coming home to YOU!